D0021407

Presented to:

Chris Newman

From:

Alice

Date:

2007

Copyright © 2006 by Mark Gilroy Communications, Franklin, Tennessee
www.markgilroy.com

Published by J. Countryman, a division of Thomas Nelson, Inc., Nashville, Tennessee 37214

Written by: Mark K. Gilroy
Managing editor: Jessica Inman

All rights reserved. No portion of this publication may be reproduced, stored in a retrieval system
or transmitted in any form by any means—electronic, mechanical, photocopying, recording, or any other—
except for brief quotations in printed reviews, without the prior written permission of the publisher.

Unless otherwise indicated, Scripture quotations are taken from *The Holy Bible, New Century Version*,
copyright © 1987, 1988, 1991 by Word Publishing, Dallas, Texas 75039. Used by permission.

Scriptures marked NKJV are taken from *The New King James Version*.
Copyright © 1979, 1980, 1982, Thomas Nelson, Inc.

Scripture quotations marked NLT are taken from the *Holy Bible, New Living Translation*, copyright © 1996.
Used by permission of Tyndale House Publishers, Inc., Wheaton, Illinois 60189. All rights reserved.

www.jcountryman.com
www.thomasnelson.com

Designed by Thinkpen Design LLC, Springdale, Arkansas

ISBN 1-4041-0357-0

Printed and bound in the United States of America

Streams *of* Grace

SIMPLE WORDS *of* ASSURANCE *to*
EXPERIENCE GOD'S LOVE *in* YOUR HEART

God's Favor to You

INTRODUCTION

Grace comes to us not because of what we have accomplished or earned but because God *favors* us.

His favor toward you is the very source of your life and your every blessing. His favor is expressed most fully in the gift of His Son Jesus Christ, to offer you the salvation you could have no other way.

We sometimes look at others and wonder how it is that they are so favored in life. But today, as you experience the words and images of *Streams of Grace*, celebrate and cherish God's favor toward you.

Leave the broken,
irreversible past in God's hands,
and step out into the invincible
future with Him.

OSWALD CHAMBERS

Grace means
that God loves us
no matter what
is in our *past.*

God did not begin His search
for you when you had finally
started home after years
of turning your back on Him.
No, His search for you
began the moment the
back door slammed shut
as you ran from the home
of your true heart.

Is it possible that I sinned so greatly and fought
against God so mightily out of pure, simple fear?

Fear of never measuring up and
living out a true walk of faith?

Receiving His forgiveness truly is the greatest blessing
and most life-transforming moment in one's life.
It is only then that we are freed from the shackles
of fear, rejection, despair, and regret.

God always takes the initiative.

We need never wonder if He will respond

to our cry for help—for He has offered

to help long before the cry was

ever formed on our lips.

He loves you so much that He gave

himself to you before you were even

ready to receive such a gift.

God tells us that
He knows all things
and sees all things.
But what is even more
wondrous about God
is that He also tells us
that He will remember
our sins no more.

15

He has taken our sins

away from us as far

as the east is from west.

PSALM 103:12

Open your hearts
to the love God instills.
God loves you tenderly.
What He gives you is not
to be kept under lock and
key but to be shared.

MOTHER TERESA

Grace is something
we experience more
fully as we *share* it
with others.

In Jesus' parable of the Prodigal Son, we discover that one need not work in a pig sty to have a piggy attitude.

When your younger brother—that prodigal in your life—receives the golden ring, a coat of honor, a feast fit for a prince, all out of your Father's love, don't miss even a moment—not a single second—of the celebration by harboring feelings of resentment or unfairness.

Join the party and celebrate the wonder of grace.

We hurry on our way, carefully avoiding eye contact with the bum on the street, the annoying coworker, the child begging for attention, always fearful of being trapped in an exchange we want no part in.

We hurry on our way to our next activity and appointment, and wonder why we're not happy.

Then one day, we slow down and offer a word of encouragement, providing someone with hope, assurance, and faith. We wonder how we could have missed how simple happiness really is.

Grace multiplies
in your life
when you share
it with others.

God will not
withhold His grace
from you because
you are stingy
with others.

But it is probable that
you will miss seeing much
of the grace that abounds
all around you until you
open your heart to others.

Get along with each other,
and forgive each other.
If someone does wrong to
you, forgive that person
because the Lord forgave you.

COLOSSIANS 3:13

God's power under us,

in us, surging through us,

is exactly what turns

dependence into unforgettable

experiences of completeness.

BRUCE WILKINSON

Receiving grace
isn't about trying harder,
but *trusting* more.

Your child does not wonder why you should be

so kind as to provide food, shelter, and clothing.

No four-year-old has ever asked if he might get a job

in order to pay his share of the rent.

But children do get bright eyes and wrap their little

arms around Mommy or Daddy and say, "Thank you."

Have you hugged your Heavenly Father today?

To speak of grace
often leaves us struggling
for words. For what we
most like to talk about is
ourselves and our acts of
virtue. But when speaking
of true grace, life-changing
grace, God's grace, we
always return to speaking
about what God has
done—not ourselves.

It was the philosopher and
mathematician, Blaise Pascal,
who said, "I searched for God
until He found me."

Grace is that glorious moment
when, after wondering if God
would ever and could ever
accept us, we discover He had
embraced us before the question
even entered our hearts.

For by grace you have been

saved through faith, and

that not of yourselves; it is

the gift of God, not of works,

lest anyone should boast.

EPHESIANS 2:8-9 NKJV

When we won't let ourselves
be held in the midst of our messes
by God who loves us and made us,
we miss the unspeakable joy of knowing
that we are truly His beloved.

DEBORAH NEWMAN

Grace must be received and accepted in order to be experienced.

A rich man prepared a marvelous feast

and party for a list of his closest friends.

After the banquet had been set and the musicians

had tuned their instruments, no one showed up. But

the sumptuous spread did not go to waste as he

found others who were receptive to his generosity.

You've been invited to a gala thrown by the King of Kings.

Will you attend?

Sometimes we shy away
from grace, feeling undeserving.
And we're right. We don't
deserve His grace. But even if
you do a thousand good deeds
today, you shall still be in the
same place, ever undeserving.

No matter.

For God wants to bless us with
His presence, joy, and provision.

Water is a blessing.
When the earth drinks,
things grow. When you
are thirsty, the best thing
to do is not to discuss
water or examine its
benefits; the best thing
to do is drink.

ROY LESSIN

No matter what your
challenge today, God's grace
is sufficient for you to
complete your task. When
viewed in such light,
difficulties become
divine compliments—for
God will never allow more
to be lain on us than
we can bear.

You will know that you have been truly touched by grace when you don't *have* to be different—but you *want* to be different.

*As you received Christ Jesus
the Lord, so continue to live in him.
Keep your roots deep in him and
have your lives built on him.
Be strong in the faith, just
as you were taught, and
always be thankful.*

COLOSSIANS 2:6-7

Every day is a new beginning.
Treat it that way. Stay away
from what might have been,
and look at what can be.

MARSHA PETRIE SUE

Grace means

and a bright future.

God blesses you freely

because you're His child.

He doesn't try to space out

blessings with bad things

to keep you from enjoying

too much—he wants

your life to be good.

We know that our future is bright and sure

because God has given us the gift of hope.

Hope is the same gift given to Joseph in a prison cell

for a crime he did not commit, and that energized his

faith and spirit so that he could save his people—and

the very brothers who once betrayed him.

Hope is the fuel for your journey to the

delightful tomorrow God has planned for you.

What a marvelous new day when strife is replaced
with peace ... when harshness gives way to kindness ...
when grudges and grievances melt into forgiveness and
reconciliation ... when indifference and complacency
are slain by care and action ... when guilt dissipates
in the bright light of a new heart ... when avarice
is eradicated by a joyful spirit of generosity ...

What a marvelous new day
when grace enters your life.

I wanted a lighter load, but God wanted me
to have stronger shoulders. I wanted gentle slopes,
but God wanted me to have the strength and stamina
to scale mountains. I wanted easy answers, but God
wanted me to have a keen and resourceful mind.

I'm so thankful that God loves me enough to favor me
with opportunities to stretch and grow and to fully
be the person He created me to be.

*Look at the new thing I am
going to do. It is already
happening. Don't you see it?
I will make a road
in the desert and rivers
in the dry land.*

ISAIAH 43:19

Nothing can separate you

from God's love, absolutely nothing.

God is enough for time,

God is enough for eternity.

God is enough!

HANNAH WHITALL SMITH

Grace is more powerful,
more enduring than any
circumstance of life.

Even the Lord Jesus Christ asked that He not

have to drink from the cup of suffering as He prayed

to His Father in the darkness of Gethsemane.

We need not seek trouble or woe to prove our love

for God. But be assured, when God does ask you walk

through the valley of pain and sacrifice, His Presence

will be with you each step of the way, and His

glorious words, "Well done," await you for

having prayed, "Not my will, but His."

When your world is dark and you are tempted
to succumb to despair, grace is that single,
flickering light in the distance that reminds us
we are never truly alone or forsaken.

And we know that all things work together
for good to those who love God, to those
who are the called according to His purpose.

ROMANS 8:28 NKJV

Dear Heavenly Father,

Thank You for favoring me with Your love, for
calling me Your child. Help me to always be open
and receptive to Your love for me and Your direction
for my life. Give me a heart of gratitude, O God, and
remind me of Your goodness and lovingkindness.

Lord, I pray for Your continued Presence in my
life. I lift my needs to You knowing that You lavish
grace on Your children. Thank You, Lord, for being
all I need—and so much more.

Amen.

For the past 12 years, Green Hill Productions has been the leader in creating music from quality instrumentals to exclusive compilations of legendary artists for all of our customers to enjoy. To find out more about our products or to locate a store near you, contact us at 1 (800) 972-5900 or check us out on the internet at www.greenhillmusic.com. Thanks to our valued partnership with Thomas Nelson, it is a pleasure to offer our music for your listening pleasure. Enjoy and have an inspiring read!

Sam Levine has given color and expression to a wide variety of artists' tracks, including Amy Grant, the Neville Brothers, Vince Gill and Michael McDonald.

Sam has more than 10 artist CD's in the smooth jazz and contemporary Christian genres. He has been nominated three times for a Dove Award and played on at least two Grammy Award winning recordings.

Sam continues to be an active studio musician, but he also leads a band called "City Lights" that is popular for wedding receptions and business conventions.

Violinist **David Davidson** has performed around the world as concertmaster, soloist, and chamber musician. Currently, David is the concertmaster of The Tennessee Summer Symphony and The Nashville Chamber Orchestra. He's also a member of The Nashville String Machine, the prestigious studio orchestra that records for the most major artists in the Nashville music community.

David's passionate violin playing can be heard on the hugely successful hymns projects by Michael W. Smith and recordings by Twila Paris and Third Day.